The Agile Leader
Navigating Uncertainty and Embracing Change with Confidence

Joshua Luberisse

Fortis Novum Mundum

Copyright © 2023 Fortis Novum Mundum

All rights reserved

The characters and events portrayed in this book are fictitious. Any similarity to real persons, living or dead, is coincidental and not intended by the author.

No part of this book may be reproduced, or stored in a retrieval system, or transmitted in any form or by any means, electronic, mechanical, photocopying, recording, or otherwise, without express written permission of the publisher.

Cover page designed by Fortis Novum Mundum

"Keep this Book of the Law always on your lips; meditate on it day and night, so that you may be careful to do everything written in it. Then you will be prosperous and successful. Have I not commanded you? Be strong and courageous. Do not be afraid; do not be discouraged, for the Lord your God will be with you wherever you go."
Joshua 1: 8-9

CONTENTS

Title Page
Copyright
Epigraph
Introduction
Preface
Chapter 1: The Agile Mindset 4
Chapter 2: Navigating Uncertainty 9
Chapter 3: Leading with Emotional Intelligence 11
Chapter 4: Building and Leading High-Performance Teams 17
Chapter 5: Implementing Agile Methodologies 20
Chapter 6: Agile Leadership in Practice 25
Conclusion: References and Further Reading 27
Epilogue 28
About The Author 30

INTRODUCTION

Leadership is a critical aspect of success in today's rapidly changing business environment. The ability to respond quickly to new challenges and opportunities, manage emotions, build strong relationships, and communicate effectively are essential skills for leaders in any industry. But what sets great leaders apart is their ability to adapt and embrace change with confidence.

That's where agile leadership comes in. Agile leaders are characterized by their adaptability, resilience, and ability to navigate uncertainty and change with ease. They are equipped to lead high-performance teams, foster collaboration and innovation, and drive continuous improvement. They are also skilled in the art of emotional intelligence, effective communication, and relationship building.

In this book, The Agile Leader: Navigating Uncertainty and Embracing Change with Confidence, we explore the principles of agile leadership and how they can be applied to real-world situations. Through a combination of research, real-life examples, and actionable steps, we provide you with a roadmap for developing your own leadership skills and becoming a more effective and adaptive leader.

Whether you're a seasoned leader or just starting out, this book is designed to help you cultivate the skills you need to succeed in today's rapidly changing business landscape. We cover topics such as:

- Understanding agile principles and how to implement them in your organization
- Navigating uncertainty and embracing change with confidence

- Leading with emotional intelligence and managing emotions
- Building and leading high-performance teams
- Communicating effectively in challenging situations
- Avoiding common pitfalls and ensuring successful implementation

So if you're ready to take your leadership skills to the next level, pick up a copy of The Agile Leader and start your journey to becoming a more adaptive, confident, and effective leader today!

PREFACE

Leadership is not just a position; it's a mindset and a set of skills that can be developed and honed over time. As a leader, you face a constant stream of challenges and opportunities, and it's essential to be equipped to handle both with agility and confidence. The Agile Leader: Navigating Uncertainty and Embracing Change with Confidence is designed to help you do just that.

In this book, you'll find a wealth of practical advice and actionable steps for developing your leadership skills and building a more effective and adaptable leadership style. You'll learn about the principles of agile leadership, including emotional intelligence, relationship building, and team management. You'll also discover the benefits of implementing agile methodologies in your organization, and how to do so successfully.

Whether you're a seasoned leader or just starting out, The Agile Leader is the ultimate guide to becoming a more confident, effective, and adaptive leader. With its engaging writing style, real-life examples, and actionable steps, this book is designed to be a valuable resource for anyone looking to improve their leadership skills and achieve their full potential.

So if you're ready to become a more agile, confident, and effective leader, pick up a copy of The Agile Leader today. Whether you're leading a team, running a business, or simply looking to enhance your own personal and professional growth, this book has something to offer. Let's get started!

The Agile Leader: Navigating Uncertainty and Embracing Change with Confidence

BY

Josh Luberisse

TABLE OF CONTENTS

Chapter 1: The Agile Mindset
- *Understanding Agile Principles*
- *The Importance of Adaptability in Leadership*

- *Embracing Change and Empowering Your Team*

Chapter 2: Navigating Uncertainty
- *Identifying and Managing Risk*
- *Strategies for Decision Making in Unpredictable Situations*
- *Building Resilience in Yourself and Your Team*

Chapter 3: Leading with Emotional Intelligence
- *The Importance of Self-Awareness in Leadership*
- *Managing Emotions and Building Strong Relationships*
- *Communicating Effectively in Challenging Situations*

Chapter 4: Building and Leading High-Performance Teams
- *Creating a Shared Vision and Values*
- *Fostering Collaboration and Innovation*
- *Developing a Culture of Continuous Improvement*

Chapter 5: Implementing Agile Methodologies
- *Scrum, Kanban, and other Agile frameworks*
- *Overcoming Resistance to Change*
- *Measuring and Improving Agile Performance*

Chapter 6: Agile Leadership in Practice
- *Case studies of Agile Leaders and Organizations*
- *Common Pitfalls and How to Avoid Them*
- *Actionable Steps for Implementing Agile Leadership in Your Organization*

Conclusion
- *References and Further Reading*

CHAPTER 1: THE AGILE MINDSET

In today's fast-paced and ever-changing business environment, leaders must be able to adapt and respond quickly to new challenges and opportunities. The Agile mindset is a way of thinking and working that emphasizes flexibility, speed, and continuous improvement. By embracing the Agile mindset, leaders can become more effective at navigating uncertainty, empowering their teams, and driving results.

Understanding Agile Principles
The Agile mindset is based on a set of principles outlined in the Agile Manifesto. These principles include:

- Individuals and interactions take precedence over processes and tool
- Prioritizing working software over comprehensive documentation
- Putting an emphasis on collaborating with customers rather than negotiating contracts
- Adapting to changing conditions rather than strictly adhering to a plan

These guiding principles place an emphasis on the contribution of individuals, functional software, and cooperative efforts from customers in order to achieve success. They also highlight the importance of being flexible and having the ability to adapt to changing circumstances. Adopting these guiding principles enables leaders to establish a culture of continuous improvement within their organizations, which in turn enables those organizations' teams to adjust to new circumstances and seize new opportunities.

Consider a company that develops software for the healthcare industry, for instance. Historically, the company's development process relied heavily on detailed documentation and a rigid development schedule. Nonetheless, as the healthcare industry evolved rapidly, the company struggled to keep up with new regulations and shifting customer demands. By adopting an Agile development process, the company was able to respond to market changes more quickly and create software that satisfied customer requirements. The team was able to collaborate more effectively, focusing on delivering functional software and incorporating customer feedback throughout the development process. This resulted in a substantial increase in customer satisfaction and a significant improvement in the company's bottom line.

Another example is a retail company whose sales were declining. In order to remain competitive, the company's leaders realized they needed to respond more quickly to market changes. Using an Agile methodology, they prioritized delivering working software and incorporating customer feedback throughout the entire development process. This resulted in a substantial increase in customer satisfaction and a significant improvement in the company's bottom line.

Leaders who adopt Agile principles can anticipate a number of benefits. Leaders can create a more productive and engaged workforce by focusing on individuals and interactions. By concentrating on functional software, leaders can ensure that their teams provide value to customers. By emphasizing customer collaboration, leaders can ensure that their teams develop products and services that meet customer needs. And by focusing on change response, leaders can foster a culture of innovation and continuous improvement that enables their teams to adapt to new challenges and seize new opportunities.

Agile principles are a way of thinking and working that prioritizes adaptability, velocity, and continuous improvement. By embracing Agile principles, leaders can foster a culture of continuous improvement that enables their teams to adapt to new opportunities and challenges. In the following chapter, we will examine the strategies and techniques leaders can employ to navigate uncertainty and build resilience within themselves and their teams.

The Importance of Adaptability in Agile Leadership

Leaders must be able to respond rapidly to new challenges and opportunities in today's rapidly changing business environment. Adaptability is crucial to success because it enables leaders to navigate uncertainty and remain ahead of the competition. In addition to being able to change course when necessary, adaptability involves being receptive to new ideas, perspectives, and methods of operation. It requires resiliency, adaptability, and the courage to take calculated risks.

Technology is an industry where adaptability is particularly important. The technology industry is in a constant state of change, and its leaders must be able to quickly adapt to new developments and emerging trends. A company that specializes in developing software for mobile devices, for instance, must be able to adapt to market shifts, such as the rise of smartphones and tablets and the decline of traditional feature phones. Through adaptability, the company can stay ahead of the curve and continue to provide customers with value.

The retail industry is another sector where flexibility is crucial. The retail industry faces a number of obstacles, including the rise of e-commerce and consumers' shifting preferences. To remain competitive, retail industry leaders must be able to adapt to these changes, such as by establishing an online presence and adopting new technologies. A retail company that specializes in fashion, for instance, must be able to adapt to changing trends and styles and deliver what their customers require in a timely manner.

In the field of healthcare, adaptability is also an extremely valuable quality to possess. The healthcare industry faces a number of obstacles, including an aging population, rising healthcare costs, and shifting regulations. Leaders in the healthcare industry must be able to adapt to these changes in order to continue providing high-quality care to patients and maintaining their financial viability. A hospital that specializes in oncology, for instance, must be able to adapt to the latest research and development in oncology and provide the best possible care to its patients.

To summarize, adaptability is a critical leadership skill in today's rapidly changing business environment.

Embracing Change and Empowering Your Team

The Agile mindset emphasizes being open to new experiences and giving members of your team more responsibility. As a leader, one of the most important things you can do is acknowledge the fact that change is unavoidable and that it presents a chance for expansion and innovation. You can foster a culture of innovation and continuous improvement in your organization if you encourage members of your team to accept change and rise to the occasion of new challenges. To truly empower your team, you must also provide them with the independence and resources they require to achieve their goals. This includes providing them with distinct goals and objectives, as well as the tools and support they require to accomplish those goals and objectives.

The Agile mindset, in summary, is a way of thinking and working that prioritizes adaptability, quickness, and continuous improvement. By adopting an Agile mindset, leaders can become more effective at navigating uncertainty, empowering their teams, and driving results. In the following chapter, we will investigate the methods and approaches that leaders can implement in order to successfully navigate unpredictability and build resilience not only in themselves but also in their teams.

CHAPTER 2: NAVIGATING UNCERTAINTY

Today's business environment is permeated by uncertainty and a inescapable pervasive air of unpredictability. To be successful, leaders need to be able to navigate uncertainty, regardless of whether it stems from shifts in the economy, developments in technology, or shifting preferences among customers. The ability to anticipate change, the ability to make decisions in the face of uncertainty, and the ability to manage risk are all necessary components of the set of skills and mentalities that are required to successfully navigate uncertainty.

The ability to anticipate change is a crucial ability for successfully navigating uncertain environments. In order to accomplish this, leaders need to keep an eye out for recurring patterns, trends, and other telltale signs that a shift is on the horizon. For instance, a leader in the retail industry who foresees the growth of e-commerce can prepare for it by establishing an online presence and embracing new technologies in order to maintain their position as a contender in the market. To effectively prepare for change, leaders need to maintain an open mind, be curious, and be willing to investigate new ideas and points of view.

The ability to make decisions in the face of uncertainty

is yet another crucial ability for thriving in an uncertain world. Because of this, leaders need to be able to cope well with ambiguity and be able to make decisions based on limited information. For instance, a leader in the technology industry who is confronted with the choice of which emerging technology to invest in may not have all of the information necessary to make a decision that is fully informed. In this circumstance, the leader needs to be able to evaluate the potential downsides and upsides of each of the available choices and come to a conclusion that will increase the likelihood of the endeavor being successful.

The ability to navigate uncertain territory successfully also requires a solid grasp of risk management. In order to accomplish this, leaders need to be able to recognize and evaluate potential dangers, as well as devise plans to eliminate, reduce, or otherwise manage those dangers. For instance, a leader in the healthcare industry might recognize that there is a possibility of a shortage of healthcare professionals in the not-too-distant future and devise a plan for attracting and training new healthcare professionals in order to mitigate the impact of this possibility.

In the end, getting through uncertainty requires a mix of skills and a certain way of thinking, such as the ability to predict change, the ability to make decisions when there isn't enough information, and the ability to handle risk. Leaders who cultivate these skills are better able to navigate uncertain environments and stay ahead of the competition.

CHAPTER 3: LEADING WITH EMOTIONAL INTELLIGENCE

Emotional intelligence (EI) is the capacity to recognize and control one's own emotions as well as the emotions of others. It has been shown to be a predictor of success in both personal and professional contexts, making it an essential factor in Agile leadership. Additionally, it is a critical component of Agile leadership. Leaders who have a high level of emotional intelligence are better able to navigate the complex and dynamic relationships that are a part of the everyday life of an organization, and they are also more effective in achieving their goals.

Self-awareness is an essential component of emotional intelligence (EI), and it refers to the capacity to comprehend one's own feelings and the ways in which those feelings influence one's behavior. Self-aware leaders are better able to regulate their own emotions and are less likely to be carried away by negative feelings like anger or frustration. Self-aware leaders are more likely to be able to control their own emotions. They are also better able to comprehend the effect that their behavior has on the people around them and are able to modify their actions accordingly.

Empathy, defined as the capacity to comprehend and identify with the emotions and experiences of another person, is yet another essential component of emotional intelligence (EI). Leaders who exhibit empathy have a greater capacity to connect with their team members and to comprehend the requirements and priorities of their colleagues. They are also capable of producing a positive and supportive working environment by recognizing the contributions of their team members and providing support for them.

Emotional Intelligence also encompasses the ability to manage one's interpersonal connections. Leaders who have a high EI are able to gain their team members' trust and cultivate positive relationships with them, both of which contribute to increased levels of communication, cooperation, and overall performance. These leaders are also better at resolving conflicts and are able to build teams that are both more powerful and more cohesive.

Leaders need to be able to navigate the complex relationships that are a part of the everyday life of an organization in order to succeed in today's fast-paced and complex business environment. When it comes to being an effective leader, having a high level of emotional intelligence is absolutely necessary. Leaders who invest in improving their emotional intelligence are better able to cultivate productive and encouraging work environments, as well as teams that are both powerful and cohesive.

Emotional Intelligence is a crucial component of Agile leadership. Agile leaders can navigate the complex and dynamic relationships that are a part of organizational life and be more effective in achieving their goals if they develop the skills of self-awareness, empathy, and relationship management.

Managing Emotions and Building Strong Relationships

In order to be an effective leader, it is necessary to be

able to control one's emotions and cultivate healthy relationships. Emotions can be powerful motivators of behavior, and leaders who are able to manage not only their own emotions but also the emotions of those around them are better able to navigate the complex and ever-changing relationships that are a part of the everyday life of an organization.

Emotional self-regulation, or the capacity to control one's own emotional responses, is one of the most important aspects of managing one's feelings and emotions. Leaders who are able to control their own emotions are less likely to be overcome by unfavorable feelings such as rage or frustration, and they are better able to keep a positive and productive frame of mind. When a leader of a company is confronted with a challenging decision, and they are able to maintain their composure and calm, they are able to think more clearly and come to a decision that is in the best interest of the company.

Emotional intelligence, which is the capacity to comprehend and control one's own emotions as well as those of others, is another crucial aspect of emotion management. Those in leadership roles who have a high emotional quotient are better able to connect with their teams' members and comprehend the challenges they face and the points of view they bring. They are also capable of producing a positive and supportive working environment by recognizing the contributions of their team members and providing support for them.

Agile leadership also requires the development of healthy strong working relationships. Trust, respect for one another, and open communication are the pillars upon which healthy strong relationships are built upon. Leaders who are able to successfully cultivate meaningful relationships with the members of their teams are in a better position to not only realize their objectives but also to cultivate an environment that is both positive and productive in the workplace. When a leader of a startup company cultivates a culture of trust and open communication among the members of the team, it results in improved cooperation and collaboration among the members of the team, which, in turn, leads to the success of the company.

To recap, the ability to control one's emotions and cultivate meaningful relationships are both necessary components of effective Agile leadership. Leaders who can navigate the complex and dynamic relationships that are a part of organizational life and be more effective in achieving their goals if they develop the skills of emotional self-regulation, emotional intelligence, and relationship building. These are the three pillars of the EQ-i model.

Communicating Effectively in Challenging Situations

For Agile leaders, the ability to communicate effectively is a necessary skill, but it takes on an even greater significance in difficult circumstances. Leaders who are able to communicate effectively are better able to navigate the complex and dynamic relationships that are a part of the everyday life of an organization, and they are also more effective in achieving their goals.

Active listening, the process of actively focusing one's attention, comprehending the speaker's verbal and nonverbal communication, and then providing a suitable response to that information is one of the most important components of successful communication. Leaders who are able to actively listen are better able to comprehend the requirements and points of view of the members of their team, which enables them to construct relationships that are both more robust and fruitful. When the leader of a large corporation takes the time to actively listen to the concerns of the workforce, it typically results in higher levels of employee engagement, which, in turn, ultimately contributes to the success of the company.

Being able to communicate in a way that is both clear and concise is another essential component of effective communication. Leaders who are able to communicate in a way that is both clear and concise have a greater chance of getting their point across and avoiding confusion and misunderstanding among their followers. In addition to this, they are able to earn the trust and credibility of the members of their team. When the leader of a small business is able to effectively communicate the company's vision and goals to the members of the team, it results in improved alignment and cooperation among the members of the team, which, in turn, leads to the success of the company as a whole.

The ability to communicate effectively is an essential quality for leaders, and it is of utmost significance in circumstances that are fraught with difficulty. Leaders can successfully navigate the complex and dynamic relationships that are a part of organizational life and be more effective in achieving their goals if they develop the skills of active listening, clear and concise communication, and concise communication. However, it is essential to keep in mind that communication can be difficult and challenging at times; as a result, leaders should be prepared for this possibility and should be flexible, adaptable, and open to feedback. In addition, those in positions of authority should be aware of the possibility of communication breakdowns and should be ready to take corrective action whenever it is required.

Leaders need to be able to react quickly to both new challenges and opportunities in today's rapidly shifting business environment. This requires not only the ability to adapt and change, but also the ability to communicate effectively in difficult circumstances. Having both of these skills is necessary. For instance, in the tech sector, where innovation and continuous change are the norm, an Agile leaders need to be able to effectively communicate the company's strategy and vision for adjusting to new market conditions and technologies. In the healthcare sector, where regulations and policies are always being updated, Agile leaders need to be able to effectively communicate new information and developments to both the members of their teams and their patients.

To recap, the ability to communicate effectively is an essential quality for leaders to possess in the rapidly evolving business environment of today. Leaders can successfully navigate the complex and dynamic relationships that are a part of organizational life and be more effective in achieving their goals if they develop the skills of active listening, clear and concise communication, and concise communication. Leaders can improve the performance of their team and their company, as well as better equip themselves to succeed in today's ever-changing business environment, by embracing adaptability and communication skills in their leadership style.

CHAPTER 4: BUILDING AND LEADING HIGH-PERFORMANCE TEAMS

In today's highly competitive business environment, the ability to construct and direct high-performance teams is absolutely necessity for organizations to achieve their objectives and remain competitive.

A high-performance team is a group of individuals who work together toward a common goal, with a shared vision and values, and a culture of trust, respect, and open communication. Developing a shared vision and set of core values is one of the most important steps in the process of building a high-performance team. A clear and compelling picture of the team's purpose and goals can be provided by having a shared vision, which also makes it easier for the team to direct their efforts toward a common goal.

The team's values serve as a guide for its decision-making and action, making them an essential component in the process of fostering trust and cooperation among its members.

It is impossible to build a high-performance team without first cultivating a spirit of collaboration and innovation. Through collaboration, members of a team are able to share their thoughts and points of view, which assists in the development of a sense of shared ownership and accountability among the team members. Innovation enables teams to investigate novel concepts and methods of operation, which in turn helps to propel the teams' overall performance forward. Leaders can encourage collaboration and innovation among their teams by cultivating an atmosphere that is receptive to novel concepts and by pushing members of their teams to try out untested strategies and take calculated risks.

Building a high-performance team requires the incorporation of many essential components, one of which is the cultivation of a culture of continuous improvement. This culture encourages members of the team to continually identify and address areas that could be improved, as well as to strive for excellence in everything that they do. A culture that emphasizes continuous improvement helps to foster a sense of ownership and accountability among members of a team, which, in turn, contributes to the progression of the team's performance. A culture of continuous improvement can be developed in an organization by leaders who establish clear expectations, provide regular feedback, and recognize and reward team members for their efforts to improve the organization.

In the technology industry, for instance, high-performance teams are necessary for staying ahead of the competition and delivering products and services that meet the needs of customers. In order to stay one step ahead of the competition, leaders in the technology industry need to develop a culture of continuous improvement, foster an environment that encourages collaboration and innovation among team members, and create a shared vision and set of values that are congruent with the mission and strategy of the company. Similarly, in the healthcare industry, high-performance teams are essential for providing high-quality care to patients and staying abreast of the most recent medical developments.

Building and leading high-performance teams is crucial for

organizations to succeed in today's competitive business climate. Leaders can construct teams that are capable of accomplishing great things and driving the organization's performance forward if they first establish a shared vision and set of values, then cultivate an environment that encourages collaboration and innovation, and finally develop a culture that emphasizes continuous improvement. Leaders can improve the performance of both their team and their company by adhering to these guiding principles, which will also better prepare them to compete successfully in the dynamic and volatile modern business environment.

CHAPTER 5: IMPLEMENTING AGILE METHODOLOGIES

Agile methodologies are a set of guiding principles and practices designed to assist teams in delivering high-quality products and services in a flexible, adaptive, and responsive manner. Agile methodologies are especially well-suited for environments that are characterized by uncertainty, complexity, and rapid change.

One of the fundamental principles of Agile methodologies is iterative and incremental development. This means that teams work in short iterations that are time-boxed, delivering regular, small, incremental improvements to the product or service they are working on. This strategy enables teams to respond rapidly to shifting requirements and feedback, as well as to deliver high-quality products and services in a timely manner while maintaining an efficient level of productivity.

An additional fundamental aspect of Agile methodologies is that they are based on a cooperative and cross-departmental approach to problem solving. This means that teams are made up of individuals who come from a variety of fields and backgrounds, and these individuals work together to deliver the product or service. This strategy enables teams to make use of the collective knowledge, skills, and expertise of team members, as well as to deliver high-quality products and services in a way that is both collaborative and efficient.

The Scrum Methodology is presently one of the most widely used Agile methodologies. Scrum is a framework that can be used to manage and finish complicated projects. It is based on the Agile manifesto and offers a structure for implementing Agile methodologies in a team setting. Although it was designed specifically for software development projects, Scrum Methodology is adaptable enough to be used for a wide variety of other types of projects as well.

The Product Owner, the Scrum Master, and the Development Team are the three essential roles that comprise the Scrum Methodology. The Product Owner is responsible for defining the product backlog and making certain that the team is focusing their efforts on the most vital aspects of the project. The Scrum Master's responsibilities include acting as a facilitator for the Scrum process and ensuring that the team adheres to the Scrum framework at all times. It is the responsibility of the Development Team to actually deliver the product or service.

In addition, Scrum incorporates three essential ceremonies: the Sprint Planning meeting, the Daily Scrum, and the Sprint Review. The Sprint Planning is a meeting where the team plans the upcoming sprint. The Daily Scrum is a meeting that takes place every day where the team discusses its progress and makes plans for the following day. Finally, the Sprint Review meeting is a meeting where the team discusses the work that was accomplished during the previous sprint.

Another popular Agile methodology is Kanban. Kanban is a visual framework for managing and completing work. Work can be organized and completed more effectively using the Kanban method. Just-in-time and pull-based systems are the conceptual underpinnings of this approach. Kanban is an extremely useful tool for teams that are working on a continuous flow of work, such as in manufacturing or service delivery.

The Kanban methodology is centered around the utilization of a visual board for the purposes of managing and monitoring the flow of work. The board is divided into columns that represent the different stages of the work, such as "To Do", "In Progress", and "Done". Team members add cards or sticky notes to the board to represent the work that needs to be done.

Kanban consists of not only a visual cue but also a set of rules and practices, such as controlling the flow of work and limiting the amount of work that is currently in progress. These guidelines and best practices are intended to assist teams in being more adaptable, responsive, and flexible in the delivery of high-quality products and services.

Kanban is a methodology that can be utilized for inventory management by businesses operating in the retail industry, for instance. By limiting the amount of work in progress, they can ensure that they always have the right products in stock, without overstocking or running out of stock. In the IT service sector, Agile methodologies like Scrum can be used to manage software development projects. By breaking down the project into small, manageable chunks and regularly reviewing progress, the team can deliver high-quality software in a timely and efficient manner.

In recent years, Agile methodologies have seen a surge in popularity as an approach to the management of complex projects and the delivery of high-quality results. In contrast to more conventional and inflexible approaches to project management, these methodologies place a greater emphasis on adaptability, collaboration, and flexibility. In this chapter, we will investigate the fundamental tenets of Agile methodologies and the ways in which these tenets can be integrated into leadership in order to achieve success in the dynamic and unpredictable business environment of today.

One of the most important principles of Agile methodologies is the idea of continuous improvement. Agile leaders understand that there is always room for improvement and are constantly looking for ways to optimize processes and increase efficiency. This can be achieved through regular retrospectives, where team members gather to reflect on their progress and identify areas for improvement.

Another key principle of Agile methodologies is the emphasis on collaboration and teamwork. Agile leaders understand the importance of fostering a culture of collaboration, where team members are encouraged to share their ideas and work together to solve problems. This can be achieved through regular team meetings, where team members can share updates and collaborate on projects. Agile leaders also understand the importance of being adaptable and responsive to change. In today's rapidly changing business environment, leaders must be able to respond quickly to new challenges and opportunities in order to stay ahead of the competition. Agile methodologies provide a framework for leaders to do this by prioritizing flexibility and adaptability over traditional, rigid project management approaches.

Before leaders can successfully implement Agile methodologies, they must first have a solid understanding of the methodology's guiding principles and practices. This includes having a solid understanding of the Agile Manifesto, as well as the values and principles outlined in it, in addition to having a solid understanding of the various Agile frameworks, such as Scrum, Kanban, and Lean. In addition to this, leaders are required to have a crystal-clear understanding of the goals and objectives of their team, in addition to the specific challenges and opportunities that they face.

When leaders have a comprehensive understanding of the Agile methodologies' guiding principles and practices, they are ready to begin implementing these methodologies within their own organizations. This may involve providing members of the team with training on Agile methodologies, establishing regular team meetings, and cultivating a culture of continuous improvement and collaboration.

However, it is essential to keep in mind that putting Agile methodologies into practice is not a one-time occurrence, but rather an ongoing procedure that involves continuous modification and enhancement. In order to achieve success in today's rapidly shifting business environment, Agile leaders need to make a commitment to lifelong learning, growth, and improvement.

Spotify is an excellent illustration of a company that has been able to successfully implement Agile methodologies. The company has implemented a novel method of Agile management known as the "Scaled Agile Framework," which enables a greater degree of flexibility and adaptability in the process of developing new products. Because of this, they have been able to reduce delivery times, increase the amount of collaboration, and ultimately produce better products for their customers. ING, a Dutch multinational banking and financial services corporation, is another instance. In 2011, they began the process of implementing the Scrum framework, and today, it is utilized in the majority of the company's IT projects. The adoption of Agile methodologies has resulted in improved customer satisfaction, improved communication, and enhanced opportunities for collaborative problem solving.

Implementing Agile methodologies can, in conclusion, provide leaders with a framework that can help them navigate uncertainty, foster collaboration and innovation, and drive success in today's rapidly changing business environment. However, in order to achieve success, leaders need to have a solid understanding of the fundamental ideas and procedures underlying Agile methodologies, as well as the ability to continuously adapt to new circumstances and enhance their skills.

CHAPTER 6: AGILE LEADERSHIP IN PRACTICE

Agile leadership is a powerful approach that, as we have discussed throughout this book, can assist organizations in navigating uncertainty, foster collaboration and innovation, and build high-performance teams. However, putting agile methodologies into practice can be difficult and challenging, and there are several common pitfalls that leaders need to be aware of in order to avoid them.

One common pitfall is a lack of buy-in from key stakeholders. Agile methodologies require a significant shift in mindset and behavior, and it is essential that everyone involved understands the benefits and is committed to making the transition. Without buy-in, it is unlikely that the agile approach will be successful. To avoid this pitfall, leaders should make sure to clearly communicate the benefits of agile methodologies, involve key stakeholders in the planning and implementation process, and provide ongoing training and support.

Another common pitfall is a lack of clear goals and objectives. Agile methodologies are based on a continuous improvement approach, but without clear goals and objectives, it can be difficult to measure progress and make meaningful changes. To avoid this pitfall, leaders should ensure that they have a clear understanding of their organization's goals and objectives, and that these are integrated into the agile approach.

A third common pitfall is a lack of communication and collaboration. Agile methodologies rely on open communication and collaboration between all members of the team, but if these are not in place, it can be difficult to achieve the desired results. To avoid this pitfall, leaders should encourage open communication and collaboration, and provide the tools and resources needed to make this happen.

To implement agile leadership in your organization, there are several actionable steps that you can take. The first step is to conduct a thorough assessment of your current leadership approach and pinpoint the areas in which adopting an agile approach would be beneficial. The next step is to develop a clear plan for implementing Agile methodologies, and involve key stakeholders in the process. Once the plan has been developed and implemented it is important to provide ongoing training and support to ensure that everyone is on board.

In addition to these steps, it is also important to monitor progress and make adjustments as needed. This can be done by setting up metrics to track progress, and conducting regular reviews to identify areas for improvement. Finally, it is important to celebrate successes along the way, as this will help to keep everyone motivated and engaged.

In conclusion, adopting agile methodologies can be difficult. However, by being aware of the common pitfalls and taking proactive measures to avoid them, leaders can successfully adopt an agile approach in their organization and enjoy the many advantages it has to offer.

CONCLUSION: REFERENCES AND FURTHER READING

1. "Leadership: The Art of Inspiring and Guiding Others" by John C. Maxwell
2. "The 7 Habits of Highly Effective People: Powerful Lessons in Personal Change" by Stephen Covey
3. "Drive: The Surprising Truth About What Motivates Us" by Daniel H. Pink
4. "The Charisma Myth: How Anyone Can Master the Art and Science of Personal Magnetism" by Olivia Fox Cabane
5. "Never Split the Difference: Negotiating As If Your Life Depended On It" by Chris Voss
6. "The Leader Who Had No Title: A Modern Fable on Real Success in Business and in Life" by Robin Sharma
7. "Start with Why: How Great Leaders Inspire Everyone to Take Action" by Simon Sinek
8. "The Power of Vulnerability: Teachings of Authenticity, Connections and Courage" by Brené Brown
9. "The Power of Intentional Leadership: How to Build a Thriving Organization" by John C. Maxwell
10. "Leaders Eat Last: Why Some Teams Pull Together and Others Don't" by Simon Sinek.

EPILOGUE

As we come to the end of "The Agile Leader: Navigating Uncertainty and Embracing Change with Confidence," it is important to reflect on the key takeaways and lessons outlined throughout the book.

First and foremost, we have emphasized the importance of adaptability and the ability to navigate uncertainty in today's rapidly changing business environment. We have discussed the benefits of embracing agile principles, such as fostering collaboration and innovation, creating a shared vision and values, and developing a culture of continuous improvement.

We have also examined the role of emotional intelligence in leadership and the importance of managing emotions, building strong relationships, and communicating effectively in challenging situations. We discussed the importance of building high-performance teams and implementing agile methodologies.

We also addressed common pitfalls that leaders may encounter and provided strategies for avoiding them. Finally, we provided actionable steps for implementing agile leadership in any organization.

However, this book is not the end of the journey, but rather a starting point. As a leader, it is important to continue learning, growing, and adapting to new challenges and opportunities.

Remember to stay open to new ideas, be willing to take calculated risks, and always strive to improve.

As the business environment continues to evolve, the principles of agile leadership will become increasingly important. Embracing these principles will enable you to lead with confidence and achieve success in an uncertain and ever-changing world.

ABOUT THE AUTHOR

Josh Luberisse

Josh has dedicated his career to helping individuals and organizations achieve their goals and reach their full potential. With a background in business and finance, Josh brings a unique perspective to the topics of leadership, strategy, and personal development.

Josh is the author of several books, including "Private Equity Demystified: A Comprehensive Guide for Investors, Finance Professionals and Business School Students","The Productivity Blueprint: Strategies for Achieving More in Less Time", "The Power of Persistence: Strategies for Overcoming Adversity and Achieving Your Goals", "The Smart Investor's Guide to Alternative Investment Success" and "The Ultimate Guide to Futures Trading". These books have been praised for their practical advice and actionable strategies, making them must-reads for anyone looking to improve their performance and achieve success.

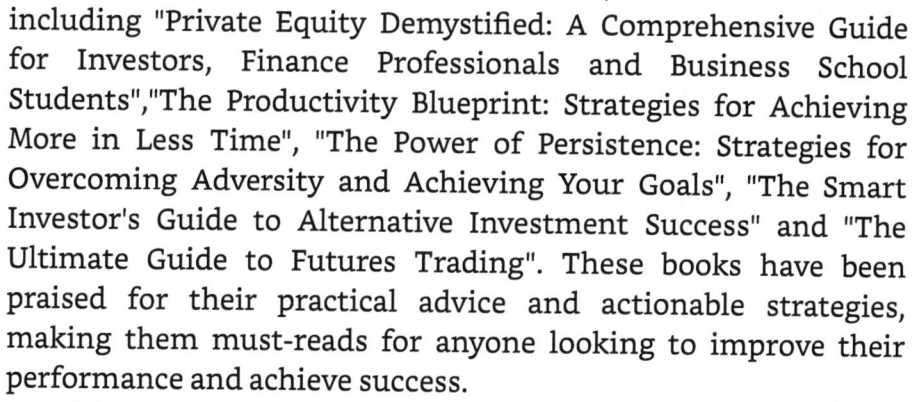

In addition to his prolific writing, Josh is a sought-after data analyst and financial consultant, working with businesses and organizations to improve their productivity, leadership, and investment strategies. With a wealth of experience and a passion for helping others, Josh is the go-to resource for anyone looking to take their career or business to the next level.

If you're looking for practical, actionable advice on how to achieve your goals, improve your performance, and achieve success, be sure to check out Josh's other manuscripts and join his community of readers and followers.

Made in the USA
Columbia, SC
21 February 2023